Wedding Vows

Finding the Perfect Words

Michael Macfarlane

Sterling Publishing Co, Inc., New York
A Sterling/Chapelle Book

Chapelle Ltd.

Owner: Jo Packham

Editor: Linda Orton

Images © 1992, 1993, 1996, 1998
Photodisc, Inc.

Staff: Marie Barber, Ann Bear,
Areta Bingham, Kass Burchett,
Rebecca Christensen, Holly Fuller,
Marilyn Goff, Shirley Heslop, Holly
Hollingsworth, Sherry Hoppe, Shawn
Hsu, Susan Jorgensen, Pauline Locke,
Barbara Milburn, Karmen Quinney,
Leslie Ridenour, Cindy Stoeckl.

Library of Congress Cataloging-in-Publication Data Available

10 9 8 7 6 5 4 3 2

A Sterling/Chapelle Book

Published by Sterling Publishing Company, Inc.
387 Park Avenue South, New York, NY 10016
© 1999 by Chapelle Ltd.
Distributed in Canada by Sterling Publishing
C/o Canadian Manda Group, One Atlantic Avenue, Suite 105
Toronto, Ontario, Canada M6K 3E7
Distributed in Great Britain and Europe by Cassell PLC
Wellington House, 125 Strand, London WC2R 0BB, England
Distributed in Australia by Capricorn Link (Australia) Pty Ltd.
P.O. Box 6651, Baulkham Hills, Business Centre, NSW 2153, Australia
Printed in Hong Kong
All Rights Reserved

Sterling ISBN 0-8069-0639-1

Author's Autobiography

Michael Mcfarlane has been involved in writing, publications, and various forms of communications for as long as he can remember. He wrote his first play in grade school and assembly presentations in college. He has written promotions, poetry, and film scripts. Specific assignments in his church over a number of years have also given him the opportunity to counsel couples about to marry, and to perform marriages. Still a free–lance writer, he eagerly joined this combination of experiences to prepare this book for those about to wed.

If you have any questions or comments or would like information about the contents of this book, please contact:

Chapelle Ltd., Inc.
P.O. Box 9252
Ogden, UT 84409

Phone: (801) 621-2777
FAX: (801) 621-2788
e-mail: Chapelle@aol.com

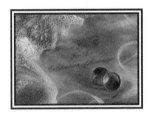

Table of Contents

Introduction 6

The Wedding Ceremony. 8

Religious Ceremonies 14

Civil Ceremonies 15

Ceremonies without Clergy
    or Officiant. 16

Vows *17*
    Vows, Words, and Meanings 18
    Vows to Fit Wedding Venues 19
    Basic Vows 20
    Conventional Vows 24
    Basic Religious
        Nondenominational Vows 30
    Traditional Religious Vows 36
    Vows Inspired from Literature
        and the Bible 38
    Nontraditional Vows 44
    Personal Vows 49
    Vows for a Church Setting 58
    Vows for a Home Setting 61
    Vows for Outdoor Ceremonies 62
    Vows for the Season 65
    Wedding Feast Vows 74
    Vows for Second Marriages 75
    Vows Including Family Members 78
    Renewing Your Vows 82

Readings *85*

Summary *93*

Index *95*

*Love is not looking into one
another's eyes but looking
together in the same direction.*
Antoine de Saint-Exupéry
Wind, Sand, and Stars

Introduction

elcome to my effort to present to you a study and primer on the discriminating subject of marriage and weddings. We will venture into the past and into the future in search of a basis as well as new and unique methods of establishing union. Early customs and modern nuances will be discussed concerning the sacred as well as nonreligious marriage vows.

Weddings have always been filled with symbolism, from the promise of eternal bliss to the threat of hellfire and damnation. Largely religious or ethno-social in the beginning, marriage has, in some places, made a modern metamorphosis that leaves it almost unrecognizable in some modern contexts, and a little more comfortable and "user friendly" in others.

The wedding is the beginning of what is, at once, the epitome of personal relationships and blushing privacy.

So, I hope within these pages to instruct, inspire, comfort, warn, and validate. And, as will be repeated many times and in many ways . . . for better or for worse.

There is no one way to use this book, as there is no one way to perform a wedding ceremony. You will find traditional religious vows and equally traditional nonreligious vows. Many will prefer to utilize an existing religious ceremony if there is more comfort and security there. Others will want to write their own ceremony and vows. This book will not answer every question or outline every possible ceremony. I suggest that you use it to mix–and–match to suit your circumstances.

Look through these pages, find the vows that seem to fit your situation, have a nice wedding, and, of course . . . live happily ever after.

I kiss you firmly
A hundred times,
embrace you
tenderly and am
sketching in my
imagination
various pictures
in which you and
I figure, and
nobody and
nothing else.
Anton Chekhov to his wife
August 21, 1901

The Wedding Ceremony

There are really only two essential parts to a wedding: the vows or promises you make to one another and the proclamation or declaration by the person officiating that you are now married.

For very simple weddings and in an increasing number of contemporary weddings, these two elements are enough. These parts, however, can be as different, as personal, and as brief or verbose as you wish. In very traditional and structured wedding ceremonies, there can be many parts: the opening words or opening prayer, the readings, the question of intent, the vows, the blessings, the announcement or declaration, and the closing words. To this you may add prelude music or a musical number.

Grow old along with me, the best is yet to be.
Robert Browning

❖

As the various parts of the wedding ceremony are discussed, remember that many weddings now select from a number of cultures and religious affiliations. This is partly due to an increase in interfaith marriages, and partly to a growing trend to pick from many traditions to design a wedding that will be distinctly yours. I must emphasize that you need not use all the parts for your ceremony, but I will try to explain here what the significance of each part is, so that you may choose.

The parts will vary in many ceremonies where there is a mixed religious tradition—or even no religious tradition, but an interest in the ceremony and its symbolic attachments, such as a Catholic–Protestant wedding, a Jewish–Christian wedding, or a nondenominational program that draws from many formats.

It is most important that whatever the chosen structure of the ceremony, both the bride and groom have some agreement and "ownership" of the marriage rites. The outmoded idea of "Oh, whatever you and your mother want" is not getting off on the right foot and may prove to be a dangerous abandonment of interest and responsibility.

I recall an experience my son had with a friend in the sensitive "details" of wedding plans. The "groom to be" had accompanied his fiancée to select a china pattern at a local department store. The young man, unfortunately, was clearly bored by the process, which caused his fiancée such distress that she left in tears with the now embarrassed young man trailing behind, uttering a stream of unheard apologies. Later in recounting the experience, the young man drew a parallel for my unattached son. The two were avid water skiers and had spent many an hour at this favored sport. In giving the benefit of his now painful experience, the young man advised, "you know when you get to the lake early in the morning and no one else is there and the surface of the water is like glass, and you can't wait to get powered up and on the skis?" My son replied, "yes." He advised, "get that excited about china." The point here is the ceremony should have significance and special meaning, especially in the personal touches for both the bride and groom.

Getting back to the two main points of the ceremony, the vows and the declaration. The vows are really the most personal part of the ceremony, we will discuss and review vows in greater detail a little later. As couples consider marriage, the vows, and the time and place may have a lot of bearing not only on the ceremony, but in the personal vows as well. We will review vows for a number of occasions, situations, and family orientations.

A major decision that must be made early is, "What kind of wedding ceremony?" By this, I mean a traditional, religious, civil, a combination, a chapel wedding, a home wedding, outdoors, indoors, formal, or informal. This decision may determine what type of ceremony, the parts of the ceremony utilized, and even what you will say in your wedding vows.

Opening Words

The opening words usually take the form of a greeting, or in some cases an opening prayer. Briefly, the officiant gives a statement about why we are gathered together, or a short sermon. For this part, the person officiating, hopefully, has met the couple in advance and can make this more personal than ceremonial and keep the sermonizing to a minimum. This really is important, because in a religious ceremony the tone is set, prayers are directed to the bride and groom and the guests feel the beginning of sacred rites. In a nonreligious setting or contemporary ceremony, this is the time to put the bride and groom at ease and let the guests enjoy this most beautiful of moments.

The Readings

The readings are one of the very personal parts of the ceremony, and in some cases mean just as much as the vows to the bride and groom. The readings may be as important as the vows for those who do not feel particularly creative in their writing skills. In the readings, couples often choose words from the best known and most romantic writers and thinkers of any age. In the readings, couples have that very personal romantic or spiritual opportunity to share favorite passages. Readings are intended to introduce into the wedding understandings, feelings, and reflections on love and marriage that have influenced and inspired couples for hundreds of years. Again, the readings may be a formal part of a wedding rite, or a favorite verse of poetry selected by the bride and groom or others of the wedding party. Favorites are often Shakespeare, Browning, Keats, Shelley, or biblical passages. There are some traditions as to the number of readings, but it may vary from one favorite to six or seven, each for a specific reason or personal feeling.

Question of Intent

This is a very traditional part of the ceremony and is often omitted in contemporary services. Here is where the priest or pastor questions the bride and groom about their intentions to marry. This is also the place where the question can be asked if any one could give reason why this man and woman should not be wed.

The Vows

"If a man vow a vow unto the Lord, or swear an oath to bind his soul with a bond; he shall not break his word, he shall do according to all that proceedeth out of his mouth." (Numbers 30:2) "If a

woman also vow a vow unto the Lord, and bind herself by a bond . . . then all her vows shall stand, and every bond wherewith she hath bound her soul shall stand." (Numbers 30:3-4)

Such is the beginning of understanding the meaning and importance of a wedding vow. The vow, in many ceremonies, is the most personal, the most heartfelt, the most emotional, and hopefully the most binding part of the ceremony. However, not all wedding ceremonies include vows, or at least extended or personal vows that are not part of the prayers or instructions. Some vows are very traditional, even doctrinal in exacting religious rites, while others are the simplest of phrases or verse, designed and created by the bride and groom. Traditional religious vows may be, to some couples, as heartfelt as vows they may write, if they have a very strong commitment to a religious belief or direction and accept wholly, the vows prepared within that context. Many young couples are choosing to write their own vows and we will spend more time on that later. These distinctly personal words need to have meaning or understanding to the couple. The vows are very precious to the couple even though they may be grammatically incorrect or seem simplistic.

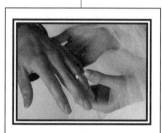

. . .I give you my hand.
I give you my love more
precious than money. . .
Walt Whitman
Song of the Open Road

bride a gift to "acquire" her. Over the years, however, a simple gold band without design, stones, or adornment became the custom.

The double ring ceremony had actually been more common in European countries and was extended to the United States following World War II. A small number of men choose not to wear a ring and there are some couples who will choose not to wear a ring.

The Exchange of Rings

Sometimes the ring or rings may be part of the vows, but not all ceremonies require rings and not all couples exchange rings. In some cases, there is a ring for the bride, but not for the groom. There are single ring and double ring ceremonies. In a traditional Jewish wedding, it was deemed necessary for the groom to give the

The Blessing

Blessings are generally offered by the officiant and are religious in nature, but it is possible to extend a blessing to the bride and groom that is personal to them and not necessarily a religious blessing. This is a time when many officiants or clergy will speak in very quiet tones, feeling that it is only the bride and groom who really need to hear what he speaks.

Blessings may take such common form as the Lord's prayer or a blessing to the earth, to each other, or a blessing from a parent or friend. The blessing often follows the exchange of rings.

At this point, it is easy for the visitors and even the bride and groom to anticipate the conclusion of the ceremony, but it is an opportunity for the officiant to get the attention of the bride and groom for a very tender moment. Here are two young people about to begin the greatest journey to which our society has committed itself, and of course, most clergy offer a blessing.

If this is a nonreligious ceremony, the bride and groom may choose blessings such as pronouncements by parents, family members, or friends.

The Announcement or Declaration

The announcement, pronouncement, or declaration also shows some variations, but try not to make this so different. Most pronouncements require some acknowledgment of civil authority or religious directive, by which you are legally wed. There are also those who will wish a wedding without an officiant, who will declare themselves married and that is sufficient. You may want to check to see if such "self" or unofficiated ceremonies are, in fact, recognized in your state before you begin.

This is the pronouncement by which you really are finally married and the place within the ceremony where the bride's parents cry, the groom's family grins a lot, and everyone collectively nods their head.

Closing Words

This part of the ceremony is variously referred to as the closing words, closing prayer, closing blessings, or a benediction. In traditional religious ceremonies, it is indeed a prayer and may invoke the deity, extend specific blessings, and close as a truly sacred prayer.

For this cause shall a man leave his father and mother, and shall be joined unto his wife, and they two shall be one flesh.
Ephesians 5:31

Religious Ceremonies

Among diverse religions there are some marked differences and some often surprising similarities in wedding ceremonies. Most contain the two major parts, vows and delcaration, but some take a little longer to get to the point of the declaration than others.

Details of specific religious ceremonies, just to name a few, are included in the "Roman Missal" for Catholics, the "Book of Common Prayer" for Protestants, and the Rabbi's Manual for Jews.

Personalized vows for religious ceremonies should be discussed with your religious leader prior to the wedding to determine what is appropriate.

In the case of interfaith ceremonies, you will need to seek the opinion of your religious leaders to decide what religious aspects may be combined.

Civil Ceremonies

ivil marriage simply means a marriage that is legally performed by a licensed judge or other official but is not a religious ceremony performed by clergy.

Typically the actual ceremony is very abbreviated, hence the nickname, but that does not have to be the case. The bride and groom can plan the wedding with some consideration for family and guests.

Every wedding should be as personal and special as possible and conducted with sincerity and dignity, which includes civil ceremonies.

Vows, music, readings, comments by parents and close friends, the question of intent, an exchange of rings, and a personal and sensitive declaration may all be included.

A civil ceremony allows for a completely personalized ceremony, and need not eliminate a spiritual experience if that is what is desired.

It is not uncommon to combine traditional aspects from various religions and cultures in a civil wedding ceremony.

Many individuals who perform the secular services, if given the opportunity, would be delighted to officiate in a more seriously considered rite.

I give all that I am to you on this day. . .

Ceremonies without Clergy or Officiant

These ceremonies have become popular among people who do not necessarily espouse any religion, but may have some religious beliefs, and believe they may give and accept each other in marriage without any noted, recognized legal authority. These weddings, however, are not recognized in all states. Wedding ceremonies performed within some religious organizations also fall within this description, most notably The Society of Friends or Quakers.

The major difference in ceremonies without officiant is just that. With no rule or structure, these services and vows can take any form and be entirely personal. They may also be simple and very beautiful, incorporating writings and readings from the bride, groom, and friends for every part of the wedding; or even inventing their own parts.

The bride and groom take each other to wed and often even use the biblical language, "I take thee to be my wife/husband." At the conclusion of the ceremony, the wedding certificate is signed by witnesses and then read aloud.

*But here's the joy; my friend
and I are one. . .Then she
loves but me alone!*
William Shakespeare
Sonnet 42

Vows

Some part of the vow or vows is often a part of the Statement of Intent or even the Declaration. However, the sincere and personal vows are that portion of the ceremony of which brides dream and to which grooms hope to be equal. This is where the bridesmaids cry, mothers wonder when their little girl grew up, and fathers puff up and brush aside a little tear or two. The vows may be taken verbatim from religious text, copied from sonnets and poems, or written by the bride and groom, themselves. These are the words that should be the lifelong promise, the will to honor and cherish, the commitment to love and support. Vows can be for each other, extended to God, directed at a lifestyle, location, philosophy, or custom. They should be the most beautiful and moving of all the words spoken at the ceremony. The vows may be read by the officiant, to which the bride and groom briefly respond, the couple may write and narrate all of the vow, or the guests may join in.

Vows, Words, and Meanings

Sacred and romantic words remind us of the need for couples to share vows from the heart and vows that they fully intend to keep. As we grow older, many of us will look back upon a wedding day many, many years ago that still shines in our memories, and we shall recall the words we repeat today and mean them with the same loving sincerity as before. In a world that can be bitter, sarcastic, jaded, and quite superficial, choose the words that you will mean and live, and then repeat to your sweetheart in this most significant of conversations.

What do the words in a wedding vow mean? Love, honor, and cherish. Love and honor, we may have some idea about, but most of us have not said we cherish each other. To quote the very specific, and somewhat poetic Mr. Webster, "Cherish, from the French chier, or dear, to hold dear; feel or show affection for; to keep or cultivate with care or affection; memory, to keep or harbor in the mind resolutely; to nurture. Nurture, to supply with nourishment; to educate; to further the development of."

Oh my, see what you have just promised to do. To supply with nourishment, to further the development of, to cultivate with care and affection. Sounds like a full–time job to me. But, what a wonderful concept in marriage. Do you see why so many ceremonies use this wonderful little word. What else should you promise, but to care for one another and to nourish, to further the development of . . . not for yourselves—but for this marvelous person you are about to marry.

Vows to Fit Wedding Venues

Most of us did not know what a venue was until television commentators popularized the word in reporting the Olympic games. A venue really is just a fancy word to describe the place where we plan to hold the wedding.

The most unique setting I have heard of for a wedding was a precipitous little group perched on the very brink of the Grand Canyon. I mean this quite literally. The wedding party, including guests, was ushered to a spot overlooking the great chasm, and with the mountain breezes stirring the bride's bouquet witnessed the cautious "I Do's," and then retreated to the safety of flatter ground to continue the party.

While not a supporter of bizarre settings for a wedding, and believing the wedding should have some taste involved with the service, there are some wonderful considerations for locating the ceremony. I recall a service in an old historic church; another, a garden wedding, with the neighbors fully involved in a barbecue made complete with smoke, loud music, and cheers.

Another memorable ceremony was conducted too close to the local freeway and when I had finished no one knew I was done but the bride and groom, as they were the only ones who could hear me.

Garden settings—or any outdoor area—are always cause for some concern due to weather questions. I had two young friends who prepared for months for a gorgeous hillside setting only to experience an electrical power–interrupting cloudburst halfway through the reception. They continued gallantly with flashlights for direction, soggy cake, and a mud encrusted wedding dress.

Let me emphasize at this point what a wise clergyman advised on one occasion. He told the bride and groom, nothing can ruin your wedding, some things will go wrong, most will not notice, but in the end you will still be married and will still love each other. Keep this in mind and always plan for contingencies.

Basic Vows

The most basic vow from the civil ceremony, is couched in the question of intent and is read by the officiant. This much, as question of intent and vow, will get you married. However, this book was written because you want and deserve more than a wedding "in passing."

Basic Vows #1

> Officiant: *Do you, David, take Annette, to be your wife, to love, honor, and cherish from this day forth?*
>
> Groom: *Yes.*
>
> Officiant: *Do you, Annette, take David, to be your husband, to love, honor, and cherish from this day forth?*
>
> Bride: *Yes.*

Basic Vows #2

> Groom: *With this ring, I thee wed, as a symbol of a love that has neither beginning nor end. I vow a love as pure as the gold within this simple band and a trust and a faithfulness forever.*
>
> Bride: *With this ring, I thee wed, as a symbol of strength, enduring love and trust. I vow to encircle you with my love and my honor for a slong as we both shall live.*

Another vow that the bride and groom have written also gives way to brevity, but it is somewhat more personal. This is a simple vow that actually incorporates the vow and the question of intent again; but there is nothing wrong with that. There is a dialogue here between the bride, groom, and officiant. This can be incorporated in a religious or nonreligious ceremony and, when all three are comfortable with the words they have chosen, becomes a sincere and often spiritual exchange. Words like trust and understand are only suggestions on ways you may depart from stereotypical language, using your own words or words that feel more comfortable.

Basic Vows #3

Groom: *On this day that we have chosen together, and in this place of friendship and happiness I, David Allen, do pledge my love to Annette Taylor. Whom I will honor and cherish from this day forward in times of want and times of plenty, as long as we both shall live.*

Bride: *I, Annette Taylor, on this day that we have chosen, stand beside you, David Allen, and do pledge my love, my trust, and understanding. This promise I give for as long as we both shall live.*

Officiant: *Do you, David Allen, take Annette Taylor who you have promised to love, honor, and cherish, to be your lawfully wedded wife?*

Groom: *"I do" or "yes."*

Officiant: *Do you Annette Taylor, take David Allen, whom you have promised to love, trust, and understand, as your lawfully wedded husband?*

Bride: *"I do" or "yes."*

Basic Vows #4

Groom: *I, Robert Allen, do promise this day to love, honor and cherish Mary Meikle, as my wife, sweetheart, and my companion. I place this ring of gold upon your finger as a token of my never ending love. I do vow in truth and honor to be your loyal husband for as long as we both shall live.*

Bride: *I, Mary Meikle, do promise this day to love, honor, and cherish Robert Allen, as my husband, my sweetheart, and my companion. I place this ring of gold upon your finger as a token of my never ending love. I do vow in truth and honor to be your loyal wife for as long as we both shall live.*

Basic Vows #5

Bride: *I love you and you love me and soon we two shall marry
I hold your hand and know your heart, and give myself
This day.
For I love you and you love me,
And love will show the way.*

Groom: *I love you and you love me and now we two shall marry
I take your hand and leave my heart, what more can I
Give.
For I love you and you love me,
As long as we both shall live.*

Basic Vows #6

Officiant: *We have come together to unite the two of you in marriage, which is an institution ordained by the state and made honorable by the faithful keeping of good men and women in all ages, and is not to be entered into lightly or unadvisedly.*

Do you Brad take Suzanne to be your wife, to love, honor, comfort, and cherish; for better or for worse, in sickness or in health from this day forth?

Groom: *I do.*

Officiant: *Do you Suzanne take Brad to be your husband, to love, honor, comfort, and cherish; for better or worse, in sickness or in health from this day forth?*

Bride: *I do.*

Officiant: *Having pledged yourselves each to the other, I do now, by virtue of the authority vested in me by the state of Washington, pronounce you husband and wife, for as long as you both shall live. You may kiss the bride.*

Conventional Vows

Conventional vows are quite similar to basic vows, but with a more personalized touch. They are love–inspired vows written to fit any time, venue, or situation.

Conventional Vows #1

Groom: *Kathryn Ann, I take you by the hand and say this day again, I am happy you will marry me. I marry you today simply because I love you very much. You have brought a song to my soul for many months. I want to live my life with you and be the simple man at your side who will try to be friend, confidante, and lover forever. You have brought a smile to my heart and often sweet words to my lips. Words that I have shared with none other. I do promise this day to love, honor, and cherish; for to cherish you is my life, and to honor you my great pleasure. If need be, I will go again to bended knee and pledge my faith, my trust, and my life to you.*

Bride: *David, my friend, how I have come to love you. As we walked and talked, we grew closer together and I knew I needed to be part of your life, and you a part of mine. I knew of no other way than for me to marry the wonderful man of my dreams, but feared you would never ask. I wish to go with you wherever you go and do with you whatever you do. When you told me you loved me and we shared that dream together, I knew this day would come, and I would stand beside you and become your wife. I promise to love you always, and to keep alive our dreams together. I will be beside you always, and will love and adore you until our days are done. I will hold sacred your faith and trust, take my hand, and we will marry this day.*

Groom: *My darling, I look into your eyes so deep and trusting, and my heart again skips a beat as it did on that marvelous day we first met. The softness of your touch sends shivers up my spine. I anticipate, breathlessly, the completion of this ceremony of love, so I may hold you as my wife. I shall always remember that moment when you answered my plea to become my bride. All the angels in heaven sang to me at that very moment. I had not dared to believe that one so wonderful could be mine, and your answer rang in my ears for days. I made a vow at that very instant that you should never want for love, and all that my love could give to you in the millennium I hope to spend beside you. I do promise, my dearest, that I will indeed, love and cherish you all of my days. That I shall pledge my honor, my fidelity, and my very existence to you.*

Bride: *Radiance of my life, hold my trembling hand and tell me that this feeling will never end. Tell me that you will always stand beside me to shelter me and protect me. The days of our courtship have been as an endless summer. The birds sing to me all the day and the scent of magnolias fills every night. I dream of the first days when you held me and we knew love must come to us. I have now given you my poor, pounding heart to do with as you wish. Oh, sir, be gentle, for I will never love another as I do you this day. I do promise with all that is in me to be yours for all of my days. I pray that all of those days be spent in your presence, as I cannot bear to be without you. As we stand here together for the first of thousands of days, I do vow my undying love for you. I do vow to be truly yours and none other's. And for as long as I have breath, the words of my love for you will be on my lips.*

Conventional Vows #3

Groom: *My dearest, I take your hand in mine at this most glorious moment and do promise that the love I have felt for you since I first cast my eyes upon you will never grow cold. You have brought a light into my life that I shall always cherish. I am proud to stand beside you this day and forever. I wish only to please you and to spend the rest of my days building a life with you. I wish to hold you in my arms and in my heart, my every thought goes with you and I vow to ever love and adore you as we go through life as man and wife.*

Bride: *Dear heart, I give you my hand in willing love, eager to complete this vow and be your wife. I promise the love I hold for you, my dear one, will burn brighter each day. As I have loved you from our first embrace, I shall continue to love you through the years. I give you my heart to hold and to protect and I vow my love, my trust, and my adoration. Your face is always before me, my day is not complete unless I hear the sound of your voice. It is my wish to always be beside you and to love and support you all the days of my life.*

Conventional Vows #4

Groom: *It is you that I love and whose hand I do now hold, and promise this day to marry. It is you whom I will rejoice to love forever, and to protect. I will savor your laughter and wipe away the tears, and we two shall be as one. I pledge to be at your side when prosperity makes us secure, and when ill winds chill our hopes. I love you because you are you, and that will never change.*

Bride: *You are here beside me, and that is what makes me most happy. I give you my hand gladly and do not ever want to let go. I love the smile that is always on your face, and the strong sound of your voice. I am here for you in whatever life brings, and will be there beside you forever. I do promise to love you and to always be your companion and friend. Stay with me just as you are, and together we will always be.*

Conventional Vows #5

Groom: *My dearest, on this day that we are wed, I do vow to love you as long as there are seasons, as long as the moon rises in the night sky, as long as children wait for Christmas, as long as birds continue to sing in the spring, and as long as snow comes in January. I promise to cherish and to honor you, and to hold you more dear than my own life. From this day forward, I will be your honored husband.*

Bride: *Love of my life, I join you to celebrate this day, and do rejoice to be your wife, your partner, and to listen to your jokes, to cheer your success, to share your failure, to bind the wounds of your heart, and share all that you feel. I will love you as long as the tides reach the shore, as long as the sun sets in the west, and as long as lovers walk in the park. You are my life, and from this time forward I will be your most adoring wife.*

Conventional Vows #6

Groom: *My dear one, today you are to become my wife; but you have been my guide and light for many months. You have counseled me and helped me. You have nurtured me and wept for me. You have led me, and followed me, and walked beside me. I love you dearly because you are essential to me. You are the queen of my world, and the beacon that shines to show me the way. I promise for all the days of my life to cherish and to honor you, to give you reason every day to love me, for your love makes me whole. I will be your lover, your champion, your jester, and your knight. No one could love more eagerly, more completely, or more passionately than I love you this day. I am yours until our dust returns to the earth.*

Bride: *Honesty and truth, my dear one, you have always given me. I can be no more than I am, and long to be with you always. You have put your strong arms around me as I have struggled, and you have listened to me. You have cheered my victories, and minimized my losses. You have encouraged me to be my best. My delight is to be with you as companion and soul mate; to laugh, to be silly or serious, and to enjoy you all of my life. Come and take me to your heart, to be your loving and delighted wife, forever and ever, and*

Conventional Vows #7

Bride: *I, Jane Ann, take you Robert, to be my lawfully wedded husband. I do so with the knowledge borne of a happy and trusting courtship. You have never deceived me, nor have you played games with me. You have been open in your affection and in your approach to our relationship. I feel very secure with your love for me and wax very romantic about my feelings for you. I promise to always respond to you as honestly as you have presented yourself to me. Even if we are never wealthy, I am content in knowing that whatever we accomplish, we will do it together. I know how richly and deeply I do love you; your presence is a joy to me, and I will happily be at your side for as long as we shall live.*

Groom: *I, Robert, take you, Jane Ann to be my lawfully wedded wife. I will promise to love, and to honor, and to cherish because I do adore you. You have always been a lady; you have impressed me with your intelligence, your wit, and your absolutely spellbinding charm. You have been a worthy and brilliant adversary in debate and conversation. You have melted my heart with the sound of your voice and with your wonderful eyes. My dear, I shall be rich beyond my wildest imagination because I shall have you. You will add a dimension that I could not achieve without you. I will not go another day without you as my wife. You are deeply, deeply loved.*

Basic Religious Nondenominational Vows

In these examples, the couple makes a vow before God, but there is also a very personal and contemporary commitment in plain words that could be chosen by the bride and groom to address friendship and equality.

Nondenominational Vows #1

Groom: I, John J. Evans, do vow, before God and these witnesses, to love, honor, and cherish Evelyn Brunson, and to commit to her my fidelity, my honor, and my trust. As the almighty is my witness, I do pledge this sacred vow from this day forth, as long as we may sojourn upon this earth.

Bride: I, Evelyn Brunson, do vow before God and these witnesses to accept this promise of love, honor, and fidelity, and in return, vow to stand beside John J. Evans in love and faith, through good and ill, and to be companion and partner and dear friend in the eyes of the Almighty, as long as we may sojourn upon this earth.

Nondenominational Vows #2

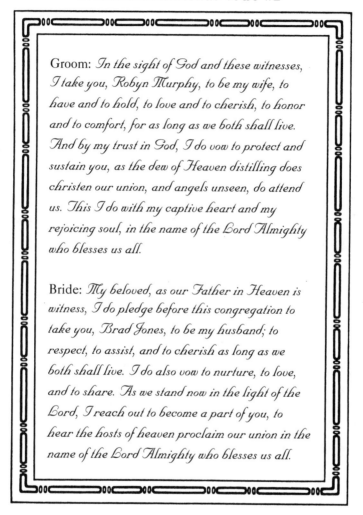

Groom: *In the sight of God and these witnesses, I take you, Robyn Murphy, to be my wife, to have and to hold, to love and to cherish, to honor and to comfort, for as long as we both shall live. And by my trust in God, I do vow to protect and sustain you, as the dew of Heaven distilling does christen our union, and angels unseen, do attend us. This I do with my captive heart and my rejoicing soul, in the name of the Lord Almighty who blesses us all.*

Bride: *My beloved, as our Father in Heaven is witness, I do pledge before this congregation to take you, Brad Jones, to be my husband; to respect, to assist, and to cherish as long as we both shall live. I do also vow to nurture, to love, and to share. As we stand now in the light of the Lord, I reach out to become a part of you, to hear the hosts of heaven proclaim our union in the name of the Lord Almighty who blesses us all.*

With this Ring I thee wed, with my body I worship, and with all my worldly goods, I thee endow.
Book Of Common Prayer
The Form of Solemnization of Matrimony

Nondenominational Vows #3

Officiant: *John, you and Naomi have chosen to come here today to gather before God, friends, and family to exchange the vows of matrimony. You have entered into this promise of your own free will, and stand before me happily, prepared to marry.*

As John and Naomi have chosen to marry and have invited us here today, I ask all who are gathered in this congregation to join me in support of this union and to extend your prayers and best wishes to this young couple as they repeat these sacred promises and do, indeed, become husband and wife.

John, do you understand the meaning of love and do you pledge that love to Naomi from this day forward, that you will be friend and companion, mentor and lover; and that you will give yourself to her needs and her comfort?

Groom: *As we gather before God and this congregation, I do pledge my love with the knowledge that my love is my heart and soul, my support, my understanding, and my affection. I will give all that I am to honor and protect this beautiful lady who does consent to become my wife.*

Officiant: *Naomi, do you understand the meaning of love and do you pledge that love to John from this day forward, that you will be friend and companion, mentor and lover; and that you will give yourself to his needs and his comfort?*

Bride: *As we gather before God and this congregation, I do pledge my love with the knowledge that my love is my heart and soul, my wisdom, my understanding, and my affection. That I will give all that I am to honor and support this worthy man who offers himself to become my husband.*

Officiant: *John, do you pledge to be trustworthy and true, to cleave to Naomi and to none other, and to make her the center of your life and your thoughts. Do you promise to stand fast at her side through good times and hard times, to give her your attention and your commitment as your wife and partner?*

Groom: *Naomi, I do pledge to be true to you, to cleave unto you and to none other. I do also promise to stand fast at your side through good times and hard times and to give to you my attention and my commitment as my wife and partner.*

Officiant: *Naomi, do you pledge to be trustworthy and true, to cleave to John and to none other, and to make him the center of your life and your thoughts. Do you promise to stand fast at his side through good times and hard times, to give him your attention and your commitment as your husband and partner?*

Bride: *John, I do pledge to be true to you, to cleave unto you and to none other. I do also promise to stand fast at your side through good times and hard times and to give to you my attention and my commitment as my husband and partner.*

Officiant: *John and Naomi, you have pledged your love, your honor, and trust. You have promised to stand by one another in good times and hard times, to support and to mentor and to attend. I urge you to give to each other of your time, your talents, and your hearts. I pray that whatever power may guide you, will indeed bless this marriage. I ask all who are in attendance here to join with us now. I take you John David Edwards, and you Naomi Ellen Rice by the hand, with my hand, and before God and this congregation do pronounce you husband and wife for as long as you both shall live.*

Nondenominational Vows #4

Officiant: *We are gathered here for a simple ceremony. We will celebrate the wedding of Cindy and Tom, and we will celebrate the symbolism of the rings. Some say the ring is a sign of ownership, I prefer to believe it is a symbol of a union that has no beginning and no end. I believe the gold is symbolic of beauty and value, and of something so precious, it may not be removed or replaced. The rings, however, may not be joined by themselves. For this union to be accomplished, the rings must be placed upon your fingers with a vow of love.*

Tom, repeat after me, "Cindy, with this ring, I thee wed, as a symbol of my never ending love and devotion. I promise to honor and to cherish you, and to be your devoted husband for as long as we both shall live."

Groom: *Carol, with this ring, I thee wed, as a symbol of my never ending love and devotion. I promise to honor and to cherish you, and to be your devoted husband for as long as we both shall live.*

Officiant: *Cindy, repeat after me, "Tom, with this ring, I thee wed, as a symbol of my never ending love and devotion. I promise to honor and to cherish you, and to be your devoted wife for as long as we both shall live."*

Bride: *Tom, with this ring, I thee wed, as a symbol of my never ending love and devotion. I promise to honor and to cherish you, and to be your devoted wife for as long as we both shall live.*

Officiant: *Tom and Cindy, with these rings of gold, you have taken a vow to love and cherish each other for the rest of your mortal lives. In the presence of God and these witnesses, this day, I pronounce you husband and wife, legally and lawfully married for as long as you both shall live. Amen.*

Nondenominational Christian Vows

Officiant: *We have gathered together here this day, in the sight of God and these guests, to celebrate this marriage covenant and to hear the sacred vows of marriage spoken by Ronald and Joanne. What say you Ronald Green?*

Groom: *I do swear and promise, as I take this lady by the hand, that I shall love and cherish her, that I will be faithful to her, that I will cleave to her and to no other. She shall be my day and my night, she shall be my moon and my stars. I say to you as I take you for my wife, all that I am able to provide, I shall provide for you. As God is my witness, I do pray you will accept me as I am, in such rough form as I am made and that you will teach me and guide me in gentleness and love. To you I promise my very life, my body and my spirit, in good times and bad and I do so in the name of Jesus Christ, Amen.*

Bride: *My beloved, I offer you my hand and pray that God in Heaven will bless this marriage as we have chosen to come together. I do vow by all that I hold sacred to love you as husband and dear friend, to walk beside you in life with the blessings of our Lord. To you I promise my fidelity and my trust, my laughter and my tears. I pray we shall grow together in love and in due time, children shall grace our union and we may extend our great love to them. I promise you my strength, my comfort, and my warmth; I shall love you in honesty and joy and this I offer in the sacred name of Jesus Christ, Amen.*

Traditional Religious Vows

Lutheran Vows

Groom: *I, Tom A. Hayes take you, Nancy Adams, to be my wife and these things I promise you; I will be faithful to you and honest with you; I will respect, trust, help, and care for you; I will share my life with you, I will forgive you as we have been forgiven, and I will try with you better to understand ourselves, the world and God; through the best and the worst of what is to come as long as we live.*

Bride: *Repeat vow substituting bride's name for the groom's.*

Episcopal Church, Exchange of Vows

Groom: *In the name of God, I, Brandon Willey, take you, Jillian Manning, to be my wife to have and to hold and to cherish, until we are parted by death. This is my solemn vow.*

Bride: *In the name of God, I, Jillian Manning, take you Brandon Willey, to be my husband, to have and to hold from this day forward, for better or worse, for richer or poorer, in sickness and health, to love and to cherish, until we are parted by death, this is my solemn vow.*

Traditional Religious Vows #1

Officiant: *Dearly beloved, we are gathered together today in the sight of God to bring this couple together in the holy bonds of matrimony. Let us pray for the blessings of heaven upon this union this day.*

Do you, John Alberts, take Margaret Miller by the right hand and promise to love, honor, and cherish her? And with her establish a loving home, wherein you two may reside, and to be her trusted companion as long as you both shall live?

Groom: *I do.*

Officiant: *Do you, Margaret Miller, take John Alberts by the right hand and promise to love, honor, and cherish him? And with him establish a loving home, wherein you two may reside, and to be his trusted companion as long as you both shall live?*

Bride: *I do.*

Officiant: *I now pronounce you, John Alberts and Margaret Miller, husband and wife, for as long as you both shall live. What God has joined together, let no man put asunder. Amen.*

Vows Inspired from Literature and the Bible

In the search for some more or less original vows, or vows made to fit a specific occasion, it seems well to go to classic literature or to the inspiring words of scripture. We have volumes of marvelous literature from which to choose. I have selected a few and hope they may be just what you are looking for.

Vows taken from classic literature or the bible can be used alone or as part of your personalized vows. Some quotes are gender specific, but may be adapted and used by either bride or groom. There is no right or wrong way to use or combine these quotes into your vows. Repeat the quoted vows separately, in unison, or the bride and groom can repeat different sections.

Vows Inspired #1

I have for the first time found what I can truly love—I have found you. You are my sympathy—my better self—my good angel—I am bound to you with a strong attachment. I think you good, gifted, lovely: a fervent, a solemn passion is conceived in my heart; it leans to you, draws you to my centre and spring of life, wraps my existence about you—and, kindling in pure, powerful flame, fuses you and me in one.

Charlotte Brontë
Jane Eyre

Vows Inspired #2

*I'm altogether immersed in the happiness
I derive from seeing you. Nothing else
counts. I have you . . . as much today as
the day before yesterday when I could see
you, and I'll have you till the day I die.*
Simone de Beauvoir to Jean-Paul Sartre

Vows Inspired #3

*. . . intreat me not to leave thee,
Or to return from following after thee;
For whither thou goest, I will go;
And where thou lodgest, I will lodge;
Thy people shall be my people,
And thy God my God:
Where thou diest, will I die,
And there will I be buried:
The Lord do so to me, and more also,
If ought but death; part thee and me.
Ruth 1: 16-17*

Vows Inspired #4

Come live with me, and be my love,
And we will some new pleasures prove
Of golden sands, and crystal brooks
With silken lines and silver hooks.
John Donne
The Bait

Vows Inspired #5

I shall love you to eternity. I
loved you long before we met in
this flesh. I knew that when I
first saw you. It was destiny . . .
nothing can shake us apart . . . I
can't and God himself can't.
Kahlil Gibran to Mary Haskell

Vows Inspired #6

Sensual pleasure passes and vanishes in the twinkling
of an eye, but the friendship between us, the mutual
confidence, the delights of the heart, the enchantment of
the soul, these things do not perish and can never be
destroyed. I shall love you until I die.
Voltaire

Vows Inspired #7

...*my dear Girl I love you ever and ever and without reserve. The more I have known you the more have I lov'd. In every way—even my jealousies have been agonies of Love, in the hottest fit I ever had I would have died for you. I have vex'd you too much. But for Love! Can I help it? You are always new. The last of your kisses was ever the sweetest; the last smile the brightest; the last movement the gracefullest . . . no ill prospect has been able to turn your thoughts a moment from me...even if you did not love me I could not help an entire devotion to you . . .*
John Keats

Vows Inspired #8

...*and yet even while I was exulting in my solitude I became aware of a strange lack. I wished a companion to lie near me in the starlight, silent and not moving, but ever within touch. For there is a fellowship more quiet even than solitude, and which, rightly understood, is solitude made perfect. And to Live...with the woman a man loves is of all lives the most complete and free.*
Robert Louis Stevenson
A Night Among the Pines

Vows Inspired #9

Grow old along with me!
The best is yet to be,
The last of life, for which the first was made:
Our times are in his hand ...
Robert Browning
Rabbi Ben Ezra

Vows Inspired #10

If ever two were one, then surely we.
If ever man were lov'd by wife, then thee;
If ever wife was happy in a man,
Compare with me ye women if you can.
I prize their love more than whole Mines of gold,
Or all the riches that the East doth hold.
My love is such that Rivers cannot quench,
Nor ought but love from thee, give recompence
Thy love is such I can no way repay,
The heavens reward thee manifold I pray.
Then while we live, in love let's so persever,
That when we live no more, we may live ever.
Anne Bradstreet
To My Dear and Loving Husband

Vows Inspired #11

O my love is like a red, red rose
That's newly sprung in June;
O my love is like the melody
That's sweetly played in tune.
As fair art thou, my bonnie lass,
So deep in love, am I;
And I will love thee still, my dear,
Till all the seas go dry.
Adapted from Robert Burns

Vows Inspired #12

. . . I give you my hand.
I give you my love more precious than money,
I give you myself before preaching or law;
Will you give me yourself? Will you come travel
    with me?
Shall we stick by each other as long as we live?
Walt Whitman
Song of the Open Road

Nontraditional Vows

Nontraditional, itself, can have a myriad of meanings. We often tend to think that we must conform to some structure that has been laid down, even in our own writings. Nontraditional, in this context, really means—make it say what you want it to say.

Nontraditional Vows #1

Bride: *Groom, to you this day, I promise a promise. I promise to take you to my heart as you are and as you will be. Your joy will be my joy, your sorrow will be my sorrow. I promise to you my life's labor, my trust, and my friendship. We shall grow together and be more in love than today. I will be sanctuary, I will be warmth, I will be acceptance.*

Groom: *Bride, from you, my dearest, I accept this promise. I take it gently and wrap it in my own, to return to you from my lips and my heart. I stand with you as companion, lover, and friend. I promise you my life's devotion as we grow closer together and intertwine as the vine and the rose. I will be strength, I will be light, I will be hope.*

44

Nontraditional Vows #2

Officiant: *William and Denise, you have chosen this day to marry each other in the eyes of family and friends. You will marry with the traditional and symbolic wedding rings, which you will give to each other. These rings are priceless to you for many reasons; they symbolize an unending love for each other; they are a measure of your desire to show each other and the world that you are married. They are made of a precious metal signifying that you express a value for each other. Will you now speak your vows?*

Groom: *Denise, with this ring, I thee wed. As we are today man and wife, I vow to be honest and true to you. I vow to love, to honor, and to cherish you as long as we both shall live, and to express that love often. You are more precious to me than the gold of this band, and you will always be my one and only love. This I promise for as long as we both shall live.*

Bride: *William, with this ring, I thee wed. As we are husband and wife today, I vow to be honest and true to you. I vow to love, to honor, and to cherish you as long as we both shall live, and to express that love often. This ring is a symbol of strength and the trust I hold in you. You are the love of my life and always will be. This I promise for as long as we both shall live.*

Officiant: *William and Denise, join hands now as man and wife, hold to one another. Be as constant and as untarnished as the gold in these bands. By your choice and by the pleasure of those assembled here, I now pronounce you man and wife. You may kiss the bride.*

Nontraditional Vows #3

Groom: *My dear one, I promise on this wonderful day to love you as you stand before me and to love you forever. Time and circumstance will change us and those around us. I know you will always be beautiful in my eyes. The gift of love is the gift of understanding, and of accepting. True love is as the seasons, changing and bonding as we go along. The part of us that must not change is the love and respect we hold for one another. The winters will chill us, the light of reality may take the bloom from our cheeks, but the fire in our hearts will remain. I will love you with the tint of gold in your hair today, and with the silver in your hair tomorrow. What is most dear to me is inside of you, and that will ever be young. I love you.*

Bride: *My love, here we are, just as we have been to each other these many months leading up to this our wedding day. We have loved and waited, wondered and quarreled, changed our minds, and then changed our minds again. But, here we are, and I do love you and I plan to be with you a very long time. Today, wrapped in your youthful charm, you sweep me into marriage. For the rest of our lives, through the changing times and seasons, we will grow with each other and still be desperately in love. I love you as you are and as you will become. I love you now, I will love you forever.*

Nontraditional Vows #4

Bride: *I, the bride to be, offer these words to you, the groom to be. As we are met here with family and friends, I will happily and publicly say that I do honestly and truly, love you. I have said I love you on the telephone, at the beach, over dinner, and in a taxi. Now I say, I love you here in front of everyone. I love you because you make me happy. I love you because you treat me well. I love you because you treat me as a woman, as an adult, and as an intelligent human being. I also love you because you are handsome, charming, and athletic. I want you always to be my friend, to make me laugh, and let me cry. To marry you makes me very happy, and I vow to cherish and support you as long as we shall live.*

Groom: *My lovely bride to be, I, the groom to be, am wildly happy at the prospect that in a few moments you will be my bride. I do pledge my love for as long as you will have me. I have loved you since the Stones Concert when you walked a mile from the parking lot and never quit talking. I have loved you since you burned frozen pizza and told me it was cajun. I have loved you since you stood in the rain with me at my favorite aunt's funeral and held my hand. I love you now, looking into your eyes, and knowing that we are getting married. I will try to be all that you wish me to be. I will be honest, truthful, and faithful because I love you more than anything that has ever come into my life.*

Nontraditional Vows #5

Groom: *Marilyn Taylor, you have been the reason my heart has continued to beat since I was a very young man. I have loved you since I knew I trusted you and knew you would always be my friend. I take your hand in mine this day and feel a warmth that I want to feel forever and forever. I promise to protect, to support, and to comfort you in any need—to be at your side to encourage and guide. I wish to always be in your influence, to feel of your love and to know that you are the best part of me. I promise to be all that I am able to be and to be worthy of your love. I marry you this day with a song in my heart, for I know we shall always walk together in honesty and trust.*

Bride: *Adam Crosland, you have taken the color of the spring rose and put it in my cheek. My eye has turned to you since I first could blush and knew a feeling I did not understand. I have come to need you as you give me strength and courage. I do not wish to have a day without you. I promise to be beside you as we proceed from place and time. I shall be part of your soul, and in time, others will walk beside us. I will be your shelter in the storm of toil, I will be your guide as others misdirect. You have come to me in trust and I shall protect that trust and shall also be trusted by you. No other shall fill my mind, no other touch my heart. On this day, I marry you in joy, hearing the meadow lark sing a song that is just for us, for I know we shall always walk together in honesty and trust.*

Personal Vows

Early in this volume I mentioned the personalization of vows. To many, this means adding a few words within the context of a very traditional ceremony, and that is fine. But also remember the bride and groom are most important, and this wedding must mean more to them than to anyone else. As also mentioned, this can be a very traditional rite if that is what you have been planning all your lives to celebrate. In very specific and traditional services, the bride and groom are often waiting anxiously to hear those certain words proscribed by their faith that will seal them in their mind and heart. To that couple, the definition of "personal" is very different and also very significant. For our purposes here, we will look at vows for occasions out of the traditional that need a unique approach to satisfy the situation.

My bounty is as boundless as the sea,
My love as deep: the more I give to thee,
The more I have, for both are infinite.
William Shakespeare
Romeo and Juliet

From Friends to Lovers

Groom: *I came home one day a very long time ago and told my mother you were not like the other girls, and I was happy you were just my friend. There was no pretense in you and you did not try to keep me guessing. When I didn't make the team, you listened to me; when I got stood up, you listened to me; when I broke my leg skiing, you brought me ice cream and wrote funny things on my cast. For the many years we have been friends, I always knew I could depend on you when no one else was there. After many years, I realized how much you meant to me. Our friendship has grown so strong, I knew I did not want to live without you. On the day I knew I loved you, I pledged I would return to you all of the trust, all of the comfort, and all of the kindness you have given me these many years. My dearest friend is now my dearest love. I will love you forever, and on this glorious day do pledge my love and my sacred honor as I marry my best friend.*

Bride: *You began as a big brother. You guided me through broken hearts, forgotten promises, and braces. You saw me at my very worst, and I did not mind. You helped me through algebra, adolescence, and boyfriends. When my mother did not understand, you did. We talked of dreams but never thought to include each other; we planned our lives and gave each other advice. One day, something was different. On that day, I knew I loved you and trusted you; and the next time I hugged you, you would know. And I think you did. My love, I do pledge now that all I learned from you I will ever hold dear. Your strength will always be my strength, and I will be as true to you as our friendship has ever been. There has really never been anyone else. The little girl you taught algebra loves you, and always will.*

The Dance of Life

Groom: *I recall a time in school days when we first met. I gazed at you across a dance floor. We were much younger, and in its own way, the music was very romantic. I was in love and terrified. You were nearly as lovely as you are now, and I wanted desperately to ask you to dance. The floor seemed empty, and the space between us miles wide. When I finally summoned the courage to walk the agonizing distance across the floor, I took you by the hand and nothing was ever the same. Today, I take you by the hand and ask if you will dance with me the dance of life. A good marriage is like a dance, you must begin in step and as you hold each other close you turn and guide, spinning and floating in unison to the melody of love. Sometimes the rhythms change, moving from sublime to passionate. Sometimes you fly apart and reach out to pull each other in and hold even tighter. I never want the music to stop. I do love you, I will always love you; please come to me in marriage, so we may continue the dance.*

Bride: *My beloved, I was so afraid you would change your mind or pass me by for some other girl. But you danced with me, and it is as if the dance has never ended. As we whirled around the floor, it seemed years passed, and we were still clinging to each other, and the music was still playing. But you got taller and the music changed, you would go away, but always come back to me. It seems there is a grand choreographer somewhere who writes our music, and teaches us the steps so that we may always be with one another; always in step, always holding tightly to the one we love so dearly. I promise I will always be your partner. You may lay your head on my shoulder and I will lay my head on yours. I love you, I love you, I love you, and I will love you forever.*

Groom: *Sweetheart mine, I have loved you from the day you walked across the playground and stole my heart with your twinkling eyes and bright red hair. In the ensuing years, I watched you grow from freckles to evening gowns, from flirty pranks to a bewitching grace and intelligence. My heart has always been yours. When we first held hands, I knew one day we would stand here together. The years have only served to bring me closer to you, our early friendship moving steadily and certainly to the love and respect I now offer you. As we shared the pain of growing up and the joy of our adolescent discoveries, I pledged to be always your one true friend and to care for you in whatever need you were found. I vow now, as I have done since the schoolyard days, to love and to cherish, to protect and adore. You are my sweetheart now as you have always been, never to be apart in our hearts. This is my sacred vow on this our wedding day.*

Bride: *My wonderful, beautiful lover. The hero of my childhood and the subject of my girlish dreams. You have carried my books and stolen my heart. You have chased away the bully and dried my tears of disappointment. When you teased me about my freckles, I loved you; when you gave me your class ring, I adored you. When you visited me when I was sick, I knew it would last forever. You have never let me down, treated me with less than respect, or broken a promise. I will always be true as you have been to me. My greatest wish is to continue to be your friend and your sweetheart. I do also pledge my love, my trust, and my support on this day which we have planned since our childhood. This is my sacred vow on this our wedding day.*

A Whirlwind Romance

Groom: *My dear, you have come into my life as a spring rain, both sudden and welcome. As I saw you, so did I love you. Can a heart be so soon true? And can I now feel a yearning when you are out of my sight?*

Bride: *Dearest one, you were at once a part of me and I knew that I must love you forever. Without knowing you when the year began, I must be with you before another week passes. As I offer my hand, it is without courtship, without dowry, and without tradition—but love tells me it must be.*

Groom: *As I have folded you into my heart in these few short weeks, it is as dreams answered, as the lady of my fantasy suddenly comes to me. For time has no meaning as love is real. We met, we spoke, we walked, I held you in my arms and all was well. The cannons roared, the bells pealed, and we must be together else life has no justice.*

Bride: *My love, depth of heart has more meaning than length of time. I will ever be true; I will stand with you for good and ill; for as we grow together, we shall learn why our love has so entwined to make us inseparable. I promise to be all that I appear; and as we have quickly loved, so shall we long endure.*

Groom: *Let me take your lovely hands in mine and pledge this day, as the gods have led us to one another, to be ever true, to give my love to none other, to stand with you in good and ill, and to court you now and forever. This is my promise on this day we two shall wed.*

Surprised by Love

Groom: *Like the child's game you play with the petals of a flower, came love's surprise. I have you of the fair hair and the smiling face, the blush of a rose, and a laugh as music. Love has fallen upon me out of the sky. Love has smitten me and bitten me with no warning. I had watched you and wished for a word or more, a touch, but this is too much. I must promise you, now, to always and forever adore you as that first day when I knew and my heart rang as a thousand bells. Love is not enough, to only cherish is to fail you. I will hold to you as my dream come true, and I vow this day, you shall never want for love or what you wish my love to be. I am yours forever, for the greatest gift of my life is that you love me.*

Bride: *Beloved we looked so long at each other, but you did not see. It seemed enough to be your friend. But my heart ached to be more. I walked by your side; we shared our minds; we talked of dreams; superficially, we were comfortable with each other. I could only pray for this day. I wished to tell you of my love, but felt it could never be returned. We seemed to walk on either side of a glass—knowing the other was there, but unreachable. My darling, I can now touch you as I have often dreamed; I can hear your voice as warm rain, comforting, covering with a splendid calm. No joy could be more complete than to know I love you, without reservation and without condition. I thank you for coming into my life. I will always be surprised that you love me—but I will never let you go.*

Not Looking for Love

Groom: *I was not looking for love, I was looking for a book to send to a friend. I asked you for a suggestion in that little book store on 42nd street. The book was only average, but I could not get you out of my mind. My life was good and there were no loose ends or open places that needed to be filled. I could cook and I had plenty of friends, my social life was quite good enough. I found myself coming back to the bookstore, not to read, but to see you; and then it became obvious—I loved you, I needed you, I wanted you in my life to make it complete. You were not part of my plan, but now I can not plan without you. I promise, this day, to hold you in my heart forever, to love, to cherish the most wonderful surprise of my life.*

Bride: *My Dearest, my most wonderful interruption. Love was not on my schedule, nor was it a necessity. I was content, I could curl up with a good book or spend a quiet evening with friends. I was only wishing for the day to be over, when you walked in the door and made my life terribly unsettled. I now wait for the door to open each hour of each day, hoping you will again brighten my day and my life. At last we are to be together, and I can only pray that our future years will be as delicious, as overwhelming, and as gentle as the last few weeks. As love has rushed us headlong into this undeniable need for each other, I promise the fire of my love shall never cool, the excitement of seeing your face will always be mine. You have come so quickly into my life and have so completely taken my heart, I cannot but vow on this day to love you forever as my husband and my friend.*

Silver Threads Among the Gold

Groom: *My dearest, we have waited many springs for love to come to us and now that I have found you, I shall not let you out of my sight. We lived apart for many years, not yet aware where love was. We were happy in another life because we had not found each other. Until you, I had no wish to share my life and my stubborn ways with someone else; but now my life would be ever so empty if you were not here. I promise to love you as I have never loved another, and perhaps had never known that I could love so deeply. As the silver has already crept into our hair, and the training wheels have come off our lives, we can enjoy each other just the way we are. Since I first knew that your grace and your wisdom gave joy and completeness to my life, I have waited for this moment. I vow at this time and this place to give you all my love, all my trust, and all my remaining years.*

Bride: *My wonderful one, please hold my hand and tell me again that you, after all these years, are real and here beside me. I have lived a happy life, and until you walked into my world, I felt I was complete by myself. I now know that completeness only comes with you next to me. I do not care if there is a little snow on the roof, because I know where the embers still glow. I promise at this time and in this place to love and honor you, to be beside you, and to give you my hand and my heart. I promise to bring youth back into your life, to love you as a schoolgirl would. You are all that I ever wished for, and from this day forth, I will be forever yours.*

High School Sweethearts

Bride: *Here we stand, face to face, you my handsome young prince, and I your adoring princess. We met with the blush of youth still on our cheeks, and fell in love as only young people can do. I was helplessly smitten by you and could not get you out of my mind. You were my hero in a T—shirt and jeans. We held hands in secret and wrote the kind of notes people in love write. You walked me to class and we looked into each other's eyes. I promise this day to love you as I did the day we met. As we grow together, I vow to always love you and to care for you. We must work through life together, and I will always be at your side, and together we can do all that we have dreamed. I love you very much on this day that I have promised to become your wife.*

Groom: *Carly, I look into your eyes and know how much I love you. When we first met, I did not want to do anything but be with you. I wanted to hear your voice on the telephone every day and talk to you about everything in the world. We knew we loved each other and, no matter what our age, that we were meant to be together. I promise I will always love you. Forever does not even seem long enough for me to tell you what you mean to me. I vow I will work hard all the days of my life to take care of you; and if we have to grow up, we can do it together, because I never want us to be apart. I will love you more than any one has ever loved you, and I will take you away to a place that is just our place, and I will protect you all your life. On this day that you have promised to marry me, I have no regrets, for you will always be mine.*

Vows for a Church Setting

This is not to be confused with a religious vow. There will be a great deal of crossover, but this vow is primarily for the setting. The vow for a church setting may be set in a massive cathedral, in a country church, in a rented building used for church services, or wherever; but will differ as those writing the vows describe and insert themselves into the setting.

Vows for a Church Setting #1

Officiant: Michael Jensen, take Margaret Ann Nelson by the right hand and stand beside her in this holy place in the sight of God. Margaret Ann Nelson, take Michael Jensen by the right hand and stand beside him in this holy place in the sight of God. Michael Jensen, What say you?

Groom: As we stand before God and these witnesses, I do pledge my love, my trust, and my fidelity. As we come together in this place of prayer and song to the Lord, I promise to love you now and forever and I do take your hand in marriage

Officiant: Margaret Ann Nelson, What say you ?

Bride: My love, I accept your promise and do vow to love and to honor you as you regard this holy place we have chosen. Before God and these witnesses, I do pledge my trust and my fidelity. I do promise to love you now and forever and do offer my hand that we may be married.

Officiant: I now stand before you and in this place, set apart for the worship of God and in the name of Jesus Christ, take your hands in mine and do pronounce you husband and wife, as you have pledged to one another as long as you both shall live. Amen.

Vows for a Church Setting #2

Officiant: *Welcome all as we are come together in this house of worship to join this couple in the bonds of marriage, where, by choice, they will become husband and wife. How say your vows?*

Groom: *This day I do promise, within these walls sanctified by daily worship, to be as this church. I am dedicated to you, my love, in strength and in plainness. As the simple stones have been placed one upon the other, gathered together in strength, so shall we strengthen each other. My love for you shall be as unwavering as the weathered beams that support this roof pointed towards heaven. I promise to bring to you the peace, the trust, and the honesty that is felt in this sanctuary. With this spirit and these emblems in my mind and heart, I do happily marry you this day.*

Bride: *My love, I do place my hand in yours and do accept your promise of love, strength, and trust. I vow, as the light that beams through these storied panes, to return your love many times over. I vow to reach into your heart as the images of saints and martyrs reach to protect us in the time we will spend together in this life. This place of worship shall be a symbol of the trust that I return to you, as I pledge within this holy place to accept you and your love in honesty and truth. With this spirit and in this place we have chosen together, I also, with joy in my heart, marry you this day.*

Reading for a Church Setting

A Church Romance

She turned in the high pew, until her sight
Swept the gallery, and caught its row
Of music men with viol, book, and bow
Against the sinking sad tower–window light.

She turned again; and in her pride's despite
One strenuous viol's inspirer seemed
    to throw
A message from his string to her below,
Which said, "I claim thee as my own
    forthright!"
Thus their hearts' bond began, in due time
    and signed,
And long years thence, when Age had
    scared Romance,
At some old attitude of his or glance
That gallery–scene would break upon
    her mind,
With him as minstrel, ardent, young, and trim,
Bowing "New Sabbath" or "Mount Ephraim."
Thomas Hardy

Vows for a Home Setting

Here, we find what should be the most comfortable of all wedding situations. We are in a place that requires no more pomp and circumstance than we wish to incorporate in the ceremony. We should be surrounded with family and guests who are also at home and can sincerely extend best wishes on this very special day. The home is still the center of most lives. Most of us spent a good share of our courtship in our home or in the home of the person we were courting. There was a time when most people were born, blessed or named, married, gave birth, and died in their home. What more natural or deserving a place for a wedding ceremony. The vows in the home might also take on a very traditional character and be most like a very personal church wedding.

Vows for a Home Setting #1

Officiant: *Linda McKay and Robert Miller, we are gathered together on this most happy occasion in this place of our daily lives to exchange the vows of matrimony. Robert Miller, take Linda McKay by the right hand and pledge your love.*

Groom: *As we are in a place of daily comfort and happiness, it is with feelings of joy and a sense of oneness that I do pledge my love. In this house, blessed by man and God, I vow that I will always love you and with that love will serve, share, and protect. I pledge within the walls of this home to be always worthy of your love and your trust. To you, I give my heart and my soul. This I promise on the day we are wed.*

Bride: *Feeling the warmth of home and family, I offer you my hand, in trust and in love. I pledge to you in this dwelling of security and happiness, that I will always love you in truth and honesty. Surrounded, as we are, by the simple comforts of home, I pledge my warmth and understanding. In this place, we shall love each other, we shall touch with gentleness and surround each other with affection as these walls surround this gathering. To you also, I pledge my heart and soul; and this I do on this day we are wed.*

Vows for Outdoor Ceremonies

Many couples select the splendor of the outdoors to be the backdrop for their wedding because it has special meaning or because they share a love for nature. It is only natural that the vows exchanged reflect their surroundings.

Vows for Outdoor Ceremonies #1

I do promise by the warmth of the sun, by the cool breezes of a spring morning, and by the wild flowers that are painted on the hillside. My love shall be as true as is the creation upon which we roam. I vow before the clear mountain stream and the utter whiteness of winter's snow. I shall be as true as the season, as constant as the migrating flocks. My love is as honest as the scent of the rose. I will love you as spring warms the earth, as the sunset embosses the mountain tops—each day and forever.

Vows for Outdoor Ceremonies #2

Officiant: *We have come together here under the great blue ceiling of God's most magnificent cathedral where you can pledge your love in a setting that will never be duplicated in all the world. Take each other by the right hand; here under the canopy of heaven do you share a vow?*

Groom: *I do vow, as we stand, washed by the rays of the sun, to always love you as I do this moment. As I stand upon a carpet of grass and smell the wild flowers in your hair, I shall hold this vision forever in my heart. As God is my witness, I pledge my trust, my honor, and my loyalty to you and to none else. I shall rejoice in this day, as the world stretches out above to call you my wife. You will be part of me as the seasons are to the garden, and I will cherish you in all your images through this life we will share together.*

Bride: *I vow to be to you as honest as the good earth. As the songbirds serenade my heart, I commit to love and to cherish you as we stand beneath this bough embellished with nature's fabric. For you, my life shall be a bouquet, ever fresh, ever fragrant, rejuvenated with the nourishing love I feel for you. My soul shall rejoice in my pledge to take you as my loving husband, as we stand encircled by the arms of this great earth. I accept your pledge and do also promise always to cleave to you and to none else and to be to you as constant as the moon that shines above, as warming as the spring breezes. This is my vow on this day we become one.*

Vows for a Mountain Wedding

Officiant: *Do you Gabrielle Goodwin and David Macfarlane, as you stand among the clouds, prepare to share a vow that will link you with God and nature in this place of majesty and beauty?*

Groom: *Humbled by the scope of this natural edifice, I do pledge myself to you as your husband for the years to come. Looking out from this scape, I hold your hand in mine and promise to be as true as the granite that surrounds us. My love for you will ever be tender, devoted, and constant. I vow myself and all that I am to you and to none else. In respect and admiration, I shall attend you all the days of our lives. To your mind, your body, and your soul, I do pledge my love and protection as long as we both shall live.*

Bride: *Bathed in the clear, clean scent of pine and wild flowers, I stand beside you and accept your vow and return my own. We have walked often along the paths of these canyons and meadows and have spent many hours hearing each other's heart. My heart I now give to you in this marriage vow, with a promise that I shall give my love and devotion to you and to none else. As we have walked these mountain trails together in courtship, we will walk through life together in trust, in confidence, and in dedication to one another. With all that I am or will become, I pledge my love and support for as long as we both shall live.*

Vows for the Season

The seasons of the year are as individual and magnificent as the love shared by two people as they recite seasonal vows.

To the Seasons

Groom: *To the lady who is about to become my bride, a vow and a toast. A toast to the earth and the gods who created it this way. To the seasons, with the lush fullness of summer, standing as a symbol of maturity in the plenty of the fields and a strong marriage—both nurtured and fed. A season where ripe fruit swells with sweet juices to be enjoyed in pleasant portions. Next comes the autumn with a celebration of creation before a long winter sleep. The crown of creation, however, is a wise and handsome woman, as ripe as the summer fruit. Grown strong in mind and body, and ready to meet a noble and appreciative companion. My lady, I vow to be that companion, to keep mind of your trust and treasures, and to partake in fidelity and honesty. It is you alone that I love and shall ever love.*

Bride: *Noble man, soon to be my husband and companion, grown tall and strong like the oak. Hewn from time and the earth to be constant, seasoned, and bold. You are spring, as a young branch bursting with life and energy, withstanding the wind and blast to full strength, bending and swaying with life and season. So shall our marriage be, ever growing, becoming full as the autumn harvest, as ripe as the yellow corn. You have brought me a completeness from living and learning, from resilience, and from want. You will nurture me, and I will nurture you, and together we will continue, full, ripe, supremely in love. I do love you, I will always love you.*

Spring Vows

Bride: My love, I take your hand this day, in the emerging season of the year. We, together, also join hands with nature to welcome life renewed into our world. As the spring blossoms out of the winter, so my love has grown and this wonderful day emerges in full bloom to celebrate our union. I pledge my love to always be as fresh and as new as the crocus, and as eager to rush into the warmth of spring. I shall honor and trust you; and as the days lengthen into summer, so shall that trust grow. The seed of love and devotion you planted in my heart and soul shall always be nurtured, fed, and cherished. You shall always be to me, young, strong, and alive. To you, I pledge myself as long as there is strength in my heart.

Groom: My dearest, you are the scent of the blossom, verdant as the early breezes along the rain washed shore, as promising as the rose bud. I turn my face to you and feel the healing rays of the sun. This time of great beauty in nature lets us dance through the meadow, share a love song with a lark, and be renewed as is this season. I do pledge that as long as I have breath, I shall love you as God loves spring. For in you, I see the pure beauty of creation; a world washed, and scrubbed, and ready for new life. As the bud turns to flower, as the hillsides become a carpet of color, and the birds fill the air with song, so shall my love for you grow. I vow to always be true; and as the spring turns to summer, the summer to autumn, and autumn to winter, I shall hold you, protect you, and love you—as long as we both shall live.

Spring Reading

Go seek her out all courteously,
And say I come,
Wind of spices whose song is ever
Epithalamium.
O hurry over the dark lands
And run upon the sea
For seas and land shall not divide us
My love and me.

Now, wind, of your good courtesy
I pray you go,
And come into her little garden
And sing at her window;
Singing: The bridal wind is blowing
For love is at his noon;
And soon will your true love be with you,
Soon, O soon.
James Joyce
Poem XIII from Chamber Music

Summer Vows

Groom: *My love, I reach out to you in this most glorious season of the year. The trees are in leaf, the flowers full —open to the warm rays of the midday sun, and you as beautiful as the sweet magnolia blossom. I pledge you my heart as full as the rising moon, and eager to serve you and to love you. I do promise to hold to you and to keep you and warm you as this summer day does warm us all. As we have walked in the brightness of the season, so we have learned from each other and come closer in our love. I give you my vow this day, my love, that you shall ever be in my heart; though this season change and the sun sink lower in the sky, to you I shall ever be true.*

Bride: *My darling, take this hand I so eagerly offer you, as all the glories of the earth are in bloom just for us. This season gives homage to the warmth of our love and light to the day we can spend together as we begin our lives in this blessed bond. As the birds do ride the warm winds and the great white clouds crown the heavens, I let my heart soar, grand and unbound in my love for you. I pledge to keep always in my heart this adoration I feel for you, who have held me and accepted me into your life. I promise to trust and cherish you as my husband and my friend, to honor and hold, and I will belong to no other in this life.*

Summer Reading

We are together now, we two,
or hadn't you noticed
that we seem to spend a lot of time
side by side
very close . . .
As now, we lie in the sweet grass
and gaze up at the distant birds
rising and soaring on the heated winds.
Life, as full as the completeness of summer,
shows us the prime of creation.
We also, in our love, are complete and whole
and choose this time
to speak of love . . .
At least I, as I look into your eyes,
must speak of love, now lest
my brief courage leave me.
Oh, make my life complete as summer blankets
the land;
marry me now
please,
or winter will come
to the earth . . . and to my heart.

Autumn Vows

Groom: *My love. As the sun sets, there is a glow of the rust of autumn in your hair. We come together in this beautiful season while the earth yawns and pulls her golden cloak about her before the wintry blasts. The nights grow chill and we gather before the fire, hands held in similitude of the bond we are about to promise. I vow to love you with all the vibrancy of the golden grain and the brilliant blush of the changing forest. As the earth pauses to review her harvest, so do I feast my eyes upon the wonders of you, beautiful lady, and thank God for his presentation of you, as beautiful as the delicate, golden aspen leaf or the last hearty rose petal of summer. Though the seasons change, my love shall be constant as the warm sun. This I vow from this day forth, my love for you shall not know winter.*

Bride: *I reach out to you beloved friend. You who came to me in spring, to whom I gave my love as buds gained full bloom and the sun rose high in the summer sky. I walked beside you on long golden evenings with the day stretching into the warm night. As the days grew shorter my love for you became even more than the bright night sky could hold. I loved you even more as blossom turned to fruit and the moist evening air filled with the scent of new mown hay. Now the harvest is done, the good brown earth is turned, to await again the seeds of spring. With the richness of this earth I vow my trust, my honesty, my respect, and an adoring heart open always to your love. Gather me into the warmth of your heart and we two shall be one in every season of the year. This I do promise before God.*

Autumn Reading

The deep red berry becomes
    the wine,
The golden grain the bread,
Our love, dear one,
Becomes complete
This day that we are wed.

Winter Vows

Groom: *My darling, I will wrap you in white fur, hold you close, and save you from the cold. I will always bring you warmth in this frozen time as we share all that we are. As the world stops and the breath of nature is stilled for a time, we take sunlight from each other and do not see the drifts and flakes that paint a landscape of stillness. Our hearts together will always glow with the coals of devotion and commitment. My dearest, I will become your warm blanket, your roaring fire, your hearth and cup. Though icy blasts may come, I will be shelter, solace, and calm.*

Bride: *My hand I offer you this day—warm, ungloved, and plain. As true as I will always be. Dear one, wrapped in white fur, I will reach for you and hold you always by my side. This wrap with which you honored me in your mind and heart I shall share, for the warmth you give, I shall return. There is not season long enough nor cold enough to keep you from the comfort my heart extends to you. There is, in this wintry scape, a beauty and a quiet that we will remember and hold dear. For this day our love and promise shall be frozen in time. I pledge my love, my trust, my loyalty; yes, my heart and soul as we wrap ourselves in the support of friends and family to whom there is no season, but hope and love. I do vow, I will love you forever and forever.*

Winter Reading

We have come in the winter
To this warm country room,
The family and friends
Of the bride and the groom,
To bring them our blessing,
To share in their joy,
And to hope that years passing
The best measures employ
To protect their small clearing,
And their love be enduring.
William Jay Smith
Song for A Country Wedding

Wedding Feast Vows

A wedding feast vow has the feel of a medieval ceremony complete with knight and damsel, yet it is a very contemporary and unique way to say your vows.

Groom: *Friends and guests, welcome to our day of bliss, the day we shall wed, and to this feast of body and heart. I lift a toast to my bride, who in radiance shall light my life. With this glass I pledge by the purity of the grape that my love shall be as true as this vintage I ask you all to share with me. In front of us is spread the plenty of larder and pantry, of cellar and granary. To she who I will always love, I vow that pantry and cellar shall always be full. Only a token of what I shall provide is before you now. I, my love, shall always be at your side, in good and ill, but I swear that ill shall not bear sway. My dearest, come fill cup and bowl for our life together shall always be a feast. Tonight my strong arms shall encircle you and my love shall know no bounds. Always I will think of the fruits of the tree and the bush as I enjoy you with my eyes, and consider a feast forever in your arms. Dear lady I am yours, heart and soul, and on this day we wed, I seek only to serve you in the sight of God and these gathered here.*

Bride: *Dearest, you honor me with this feast but greater honor do you give in your tender heart. For that dear heart I do pledge to keep locked in my own. I reach for the richness of this meal and can see only what I shall give to you all the days of my life. I do pledge that my life and love shall be as full as your cellar, and that my fruits shall be equally as sweet. In honor do I pledge to stand beside you always. My strength shall be to you in time of need, my great love shall warm you even though we may be apart. I promise also, should we so choose, fruits of our own, from heart and loin, loved and nurtured. I do cherish that which you offer me this night and do, sir, give myself as your honorable wife, from this day forward as long as we both shall live.*

Vows for Second Marriages

To most people, marriage is a venture into the unknown and met with some hesitation. The second marriage is often approached with even more apprehension. Marriages which end prematurely usually do so in less than perfect circumstances, either death or divorce. I have always felt a certain amount of support or hopefulness for those willing to try for a second chance at the brass ring of marital happiness. When performing a ceremony for a couple who have been previously married, I often feel like more of a cheerleader than an officiator. In my private comments to the bride and groom at the beginning of the ceremony, I find myself often more encouraging to the couple being married for the second time.

Vows for Second Marriages #1

Bride: *I come this day and pledge my love to one who is believer, healer, and soul mate. Who has reached to me from the crowd and offered a hand without condition. Who has accepted my burdens and encircled me with love and gentleness. I shall always love you for choosing a gift once opened and making it new. You gave me trust when my heart would not return it, patience when I gave you fury, softness when I thought my wounds would never heal. I pledge to you this day a love I did not know was mine to give, a commitment that I will always be at your side, and a thankfulness that God has sent me a person who is loving. I love you, truly.*

Groom: *I come this day to express my love for the woman I met who gave me of her charm, her wit, and her wisdom. I do also pledge my continued belief in the spirit and warmth of this magnificent lady and the joy she has brought to my life. Other times and other places are of no concern to me, I know only that I love her and I need her in my life. I offer myself to a heart once broken, I promise honor and gentleness, I promise trust and confidence, I promise healing and love. I wish to be the only love you have known, for you will be the only love I will want. I promise by all that is holy to me to serve, to protect, and to cherish for as long as we both shall live.*

Bride: *I take you by the hand and I will say, very slowly, so I can understand—I love you. I am so warm by your side, and I so want to be here, and I never thought it possible that this joy and happiness could come to me once more. You were not in my crystal ball, my tea leaves, or my fortune cookies. I dreamed of loneliness, nights out with the girls, and beginning to talk to myself. Love was just another four letter word, and I felt that I could neither give nor receive that phantom emotion. When I realized you were not too good to be true, I was even more frightened; but then the discovery that I was both in love and loved brought sunshine back into my dark days. I will pledge my love to you forever, for good times and poor. There is once again love in my life, and I will hold you as long as there is life in me.*

Groom: *Come to me my sweet, sweet dream. You were my deepest fantasy and my greatest hope. Even when I knew that love would not come into my life again, in my dreams there was you. As you are now here and real, I do promise by all that is sacred to me that I will hold onto you and keep you safe with every ounce of strength I can muster. When love went away, the thought of it became a cruel joke. When you walked in—cautious as you were—and you were warm, witty, and nice, I felt there, once more, was a God in Heaven and he had brought me you. For all of my imperfections, I will toil and sweat to make a life for you. I will sweep floors, wash windows, or whatever it takes to keep you in my life. Love is better the second time around. You are my love and my life, I shall honor and cherish you all the days of my fortunate life.*

Love cometh like sunshine after rain . . .
William Shakespeare

Vows for Second Marriages #3

Groom: *My dear, thank you for finding me and for loving me. To love once is bittersweet, to love again so deeply, is to be rescued from the endless doubt and pulled back into the sunlight. I will always hold you in my heart as I yearn to wrap you in my arms forever. I promise to honor and cherish you, and to be your faithful companion from this day on.*

Bride: *My one and only, you have come to me and given me so much. I will promise to love you for all you are, and to stand with you as wife, lover, friend, and confidante. You brought love and light back into my life, and I vow my trust and my enduring adoration until the light has gone out of the world. My happiness is complete as I marry you this day and forever.*

. . .I have perfect faith in us, and so perfect is my love for you that I am, as it were, still silent to my very soul. I want nobody but you for my lover and my friend and to nobody but you shall I be faithful.
Katherine Mansfield to John Middleton Murry (May 19, 1917)

Vows Including Family Members

The bride and groom may have the desire to include family members such as children or parents in their vows.

Vows to Include Children #1

Groom: To the lady I adore, and to those attending children with whom I share this adoration. I pledge this day my love to JoAnn who will be my wife, for whom I shall risk everything, to whom I promise all that I am and all that I may ever acquire. To Gregory her son, I promise my trust, my support, what knowledge I can share, my friendship, and three fishing trips every year. As I love this lady, I vow to behave as a father to these children that I love as my own. They will never be less than my own in my heart and my judgment. To Charity, daughter of JoAnn, I will be confidante, keeper of secrets, mender of toys, and if need be, a date for the prom. Also I promise to love and cherish this beautiful lady, so do I promise to love, protect, and mentor these children.

Bride: My beloved, as I promise to love and cherish you as husband and friend, so do I promise to love, teach, protect, and enjoy these children as my own. I do not come to replace a mother loved by these children, but to be a friend and to make my place in their hearts. To Spencer, I promise a shoulder to cry on, a ride to soccer practice, a very limited number of vegetables and pumpkin cookies. To Brooke, I hope to be big sister, sometimes a mom if you need me to be, protector from the cruelty of "friends" and always ears to listen. To you all, I vow my trust and my joy that we may all now be together, to laugh, to cry, and to celebrate our individuality. May a kind God see us now as family, and bless this marriage and this home, wherever we may be.

Vows to Include Children #2

Officiant: *The circumstance of marriage is, today, often different. Our circumstance this day is a circle. The circle is new and old, but eager and trusting. From this circle we are about to make a family. Join hands now in this new and old circle and we will seal this union like the rings this bride and groom will exchange.*

Groom: *I pledge to you, my love, and also to those gathered who also love my love. I shall be husband, friend, and father if you so choose; and I will always be close in my mind and in my heart. My dearest, as I love and honor you, so must I love those who are heart of your heart, and flesh of your flesh. Children of this union, I vow fairness, support, and kindness. I will be your teacher, your coach, and your pony. I want you to know that I love your mother with a gentleness she has taught me and a sincerity grown out of respect. The respect I have for her, I pray, you will also show as we grow together as a family. I vow to extend my arms to cover all who are a part of this woman whom I love so dearly.*

Bride: *My young friends, I want you to know that I dearly love your father. We have become very good friends over the weeks and months, we have learned to love each other. As you have so graciously shared this wonderful man with me, so will I share the love I feel for him with you. As your friend, we will learn much about each other, together with this common friend and parent. I promise also to be fair and to be honest, to be available for you as I am for him, and in due time, to earn your love and true friendship. I will not attempt to replace anyone, but to make a place in your hearts that is for me alone. I may be mother or friend, but I will cherish my life with all of you. On this day when I marry your father, I marry you, and I promise to love and support you as my own.*

Vows to Include Children Reading #1

> Family love is this dynastic awareness of
> time, this shared belonging to a chain of
> generations . . . we collaborate together
> to root each other in a dimension of time
> longer than our own lives.
> Michael Ignatieff
> *Lodged in Heart and Memory*
>
>

Vows to Include Children Reading #2

> Once apart and now together all
> We are parts of the whole and now
> Whole, but tender parts,
> Leaves of a plant,
> Now grafted by words of love.
> With the sun and dew we now will grow again.
> Hand in hand we circle in the dance,
> Petals of the rose, a part of the whole
> And now whole—again.
>
>

Vows to Include Parents

Groom: *As we stand together, I take in my hand the hand of my bride, my beloved. To you dear lady who stands as the mother of this, my chosen one, I say thank you. I thank you for giving her life, for giving her beauty, for giving her sweetness I adore, for giving her the good sense to say yes to me. I vow that I will never cause you concern for her well being, that I will indeed love and cherish her, and treat her with that love each day. She will be my moon and my stars, her needs will be my first concern. And to you, who stand as her father, I promise to honor and protect her, though I will never replace you in her life or in her heart. I will be, as you were, her guardian and her champion. I shall love her for as long as I shall live.*

Bride: *My dearest, I have promised to love you forever, and in doing so, I also promise my love and respect to those two people who have nurtured you, taught you, and prepared you for this time and place. To you, the mother of my husband, I promise to love and protect in my heart this son, who is always a part of your heart, who came from your body, whose life is a part of your life. I will give him joy and trust, laughter and solace, compassion and strength. I will be as strong in his life as wife, as you have been as mother. To you his Father, I pledge to trust this man who now and forever stands beside me. I thank you for his wit, for his knowledge, and for teaching him the good sense to wait until the best came along. I do love him and wish to be with him forever; for that love, I am also grateful to you. I am pleased that I am a part of your family and that you are a part of mine.*

Renewing Your Vows

Reaffirmation, or renewing vows is becoming increasingly popular again. The reaffirmation or restatement of the marriage vow is simply duplicating the original vows after a period of years, usually a significant number, such as twenty, thirty, or fifty years. Often the couple will attempt to reconstruct the original ceremony to the exact location, time, officiator, and wedding party. Some will wish to speak the same vows; however, these seldom fit the present situation so you may wish to consider some new vows for this occasion.

This poem is for my wife
I have made it plainly and honestly

In all that becomes a woman
Her words and her ways are
         beautiful
Archibald MacLeish
Adapted from *Poem in Prose*

I Would Do It Over Again

Groom: My dearest, I stand here once more and see you, not as bride-to-be, but as wife. My friend, my confessor, my lover, and my opponent, I hold you tighter than before, for now I know what I would lose were I to let you go. I come to renew vows and to say I would do it all over again—yes, yes, yes—in the sweet times and the hard times, in sickness and in health. I would again endure your learning to cook, learning to play golf, trying to fish, and learning to know my family. Whenever I had a need you were there, whenever I was weak, you were strong. You helped me grow and let me fail, but never failed me. I will love you forever, because you have become a part of me I cannot dare to lose. I loved you as my bride, I adore you as my wife and companion.

Bride: Heart of my heart, I take you by the hand and hold on tight. You are that one that did not get away. You were my blushing, shy, and stumbling groom, now my older, wiser, trusted friend. You are still dashing, but a bit slower; handsome, but a bit grayer; debonair, with a few wrinkles. I also would endure the learning, diapers, feeding, and bedtime stories. I would still learn to love uncle Louie, and run from cousin Ross. You took me to heart, championed my causes, and dried my tears. We truly have grown together as one, an oak grafted into a willow, withstanding the winds and rains, the drizzles and torrents. You were my knight in shining armor and now are my king, with dents and rust and squeaky joints. The love I felt as your new bride is now stronger and more complete as you stand as my husband. Yes, I would do it all over again. I love you truly.

I Do, I Do, I Do

Officiant: *Dear friends, we are gathered together again in this same place, to renew the vows and promises spoken by Ann and William twenty-five years ago today. William, take Ann by the right hand and speak the vows in your heart this day.*

Groom: *My most precious Ann, we are again in this place of worship, under the watchful eye of a God who loves us and smiles on this successful union. As I gazed into your eyes twenty-five years ago, I was certain my love for you would never diminish. Today I look deeper into those beautiful eyes, even more in love and thankful that those eyes have watched over me these years we have been together. I hold the same hand I held at that time, which is a little stronger, a little aged by work, but softened by the joys and the tears of the days and the nights we have held on to each other. Your hair still shines as the light touches the little curls around your temples. I will promise now as I did then to continue to love, honor, and protect you only with a greater knowledge of this wonderful gift the Lord has sent to me. I cherish all the days and nights you have given me, and can only thank you for being who you are, for all the tough decisions we made together, and all the laughter that came so easily from you. My love grows as I recall the happiness you have given me. The wonder of today's "I do," is the knowledge that "I did."*

Bride: *My wonderful, wonderful William, I have held you close to me as a tender boy and as a man of poise and composure. I vowed years ago that I would love you until we were old and gray. Now we are older and grayer and I could not love you more. We stood before with the blush of youth, anticipating the thrill of marriage and being together. I blush again to think of us as children playing house in a world that became wonderfully small with every discovery between us. I watched you grow and become even more a prince charming than I had thought possible, even when the armor began to rust. I am now so very pleased and happy to renew that wonderful vow we spoke, what seems a few short years ago. I love you very much and I must say again and again, I do, I do, I do.*

Readings

As I mentioned earlier, the Readings are a very personal and beautiful part of the ceremony. This along with vows, is where the bride and groom have an opportunity to express themselves. Hence, many choose words from classic literature, modern prose, or the scriptures. Some of the most beautiful readings are, of course, the great poems of the men and women who have moved us for centuries with their writings. In addition, readings may be selected from different cultural and religious backgrounds such as African Native American, Buddhism, or Hinduism. Many weddings today are comprised of traditions from various cultural or religious sources.

The readings may be brief or extended, but should be the feelings of the bride and groom. In traditional religious weddings, the readings are often taken from specific sectarian text. In this case, consult with local clergy or the person performing the ceremony.

A family starts with a young man falling in love with a girl.
No superior alternative has been found.
Winston Churchill

The essence of a good marriage is respect for each other's personality combined with that deep intimacy, physical, mental, and spiritual, which makes a serious love between man and woman the most fructifying of all human experiences. Such love, like everything that is great and precious, demands its own morality and frequently entails a sacrifice of the less to the greater; but such sacrifice must be voluntary, for, where it is not, it will destroy the very basis of the love for the sake of which it is made.
Bertrand Russell (died 1970)
Marriage and Morals

It is the man and woman united that makes the complete human being. Separate she lacks his force of body and strength of reason; he her softness, sensibility and acute discernment. Together they are most likely to succeed in the world.
Benjamin Franklin

I want to paint men and women with that something of the eternal which halo used to symbolize . . . to express the love of two lovers by a wedding of two complementary colors, their mingling and opposition, the mysterious vibration of kindred tones. To express the thought of a brow by the radiance of a light tone against a somber background.

To express hope by some star, the eagerness of a soul by a sunset radiance.
Vincent Van Gogh to his brother Theo

I can
neither Eat
nor Sleep
for thinking
of You my
dearest love,
I never touch
even pudding.
Admiral Horatio Nelson to Lady Sarah Hamilton (Jan. 29, 1800)

Love demands everything, and rightly so. Thus is it for me with thee, for thee with me . . . Our love, is it not a true heavenly edifice, firm as heaven's vault?
Ludwig van Beethoven to Countess Giuletta Guicciardi (July 6, 1801)

Drink to me only with thine eyes,
And I will pledge with mine;
Or leave a kiss but in the cup
and I'll not look for wine.
Ben Jonson to Celia

But here's the joy; my friend and I are one...
Then she loves but me alone!
William Shakespeare
Sonnet 42

My dear friend,
. . . should I draw you the picture of my heart it would be what
I hope you would still love though it contained nothing new.
The early possession you obtained there, and the absolute
power you have obtained over it, leaves not the smallest space
unoccupied. I look back to the early days of our acquaintance
and friendship as to the days of love and innocence, and, with an
indescribable pleasure, I have seen near a score of years roll over
our heads with an affection heightened and improved by time,
nor have the dreary years of absence in the smallest degree
effaced from my mind the image of the dear untitled man to
whom I gave my heart.
Abigail Adams to John Adams (Dec. 23, 1782)

We have taken the seven steps. You have become mine forever. Yes, we have become partners. I have become yours. Hereafter, I cannot live without you. Do not live without me. Let us share the joys. We are word and meaning, united. You are thought and I am sound. May the nights be honey–sweet for us; may the sun be all honey for us; may the cows yeild us honey–sweet milk! As the heavens are stable, as the earth is stable, as the mountains are stable, as the whole universe is stable, so may our union be permanently settled.
Hindu Marriage Ritual of Seven Steps

Nothing happens without a cause. The union of this man and woman has not come about accidentally but is the foreordained result of many past lives. This tie can therefore not be broken or dissolved.

In the future, happy occasions will come as surely as the morning. Difficult times will come as surely as the night. When things go joyously, meditate according to the Buddhist tradition. When things go badly, meditate. Meditation in the manner of Compassionate Buddha will guide your life.

To say the words "love and compassion" is easy. But to accept that love and compassion are built upon patience and perseverance is not easy. Your marriage will be firm and lasting if you remember this.
Buddhist marriage homily

The Fountains mingle with the River
    And the Rivers with the Oceans,
The winds of Heaven mix forever
    With a sweet emotion;
Nothing in the world is single;
    All things by a law divine
In one spirit meet and mingle.
    Why not I with thine?—
Percy Bysshe Shelley
Love's Philosophy

You have lifted my very soul up into the light of your soul, and I
am not ever likely to mistake it for the common daylight.
Elizabeth Barrett to Robert Browning (August 17, 1846)

What is the beginning? Love.
What is the course. Love still.
What the goal. The goal is love.
On a happy hill
Is there nothing then but Love?
Search we sky or earth
There is nothing out of Love
Hath perpetual worth:
All things flag but only Love,
All things fail and flee;
There is nothing left but Love
Worthy you and me.
Christina Rossetti

The Lord bless thee, and keep thee: The Lord make his face shine upon thee, and be gracious unto thee.
Numbers 6:24-25

But true love is a durable fire,
In the mind ever burning,
Never sick, never old, never dead,
From itself never turning.
Sir Walter Raleigh
As You Came From the Holy Land

With beauty below and above me, in
    the beauty about me, I walk.
It is finished in beauty
It is finished in beauty
It is finished in beauty.
Navajo Hymn to the Thunderbird

O Morning Star! When you look down upon, give us peace and refreshing sleep. Great Spirit! Bless our children, friends, and visitors through a happy life. May our trails lie straight and level before us. Let us live to be old. We are all your children and ask these things with good hearts.
Hymn of the Great Plains Indians to the Sun

Libations! Libations!
To the protective spirits on high!
To the wandering spirits below!
To the spirits of the mountains,
To the spirits of the valleys,
To the spirits of the East,
To the spirits of the West,
To the spirits of the North,
To the spirits of the South,
To the bride and groom, together, libation!
May the spirits on high, as well as the spirits below, fill you
with grace!

Divine helpers, come! Keep watch all night! Rather than see
the bridegroom so much as damage his toenail, may the good
spirits go ahead of him. May the bride not so much as damage
her fingernail! The good spirits will be their cushions so that
not a hair of their heads shall be harmed.

And you, all you good wedding guests waiting in the shad-
ows, come out into the light, may the light follow you!
African Wedding Benediction

Now we will feel no rain, for each of us will be a shelter to the
other. Now we will feel no cold, for each of us will be warmth
to the other. Now there is no loneliness for us. Now we are two
bodies, but only one life. We go now to our dwelling place, to
enter into the days of our togetherness. May our days be good
and long upon the earth.
Based on an Apache Indian Prayer

Summary

Spoken promises of love will always be part of a good marriage, so finding the perfect wedding vows to express your personal feelings for your wedding ceremony will reflect your love.

We have covered a good deal of material in this volume and I feel that each bride and groom who reads this book will find vows that are meaningful to them.

The vows and the readings are meant, in most cases, to give you some ideas from which to work. There are parts of traditional non-religious ceremonies that you may wish to incorporate in your very own wedding, which is very often the practice today. You may want to utilize a vow just as it is written if it seems to fit your situation.

The vows are always a kind of poetry that you may adjust, add to, or modify as you wish. The readings for the most part are from the poets and great writers of the past, and they still seem to be the best romantic lines. As I have already mentioned, a wedding is a very personal occasion and should define the bride and groom.

If you wish a traditional religious ceremony, you are best advised to counsel with your respective clergy about the details. Many brides and grooms are perfectly comfortable with the wedding rites of their religious beliefs and feel they are perfect for their occasion.

I extend my best wishes to brides and grooms of all ages, wherever they may be. Whether your wedding is traditional or contemporary, lavish or simple, make it the very best it can be, and, of course . . . live happily ever after.

Index

A *Church Romance* 60

A Whirlwind Romance 53

Autumn Reading 71

Autumn Vows 70

Basic Religious
Nondenominational
Vows 30–35

Basic Vows 20–23

Basic Vows #1 20

Basic Vows #2 20

Basic Vows #3 21

Basic Vows #4 22

Basic Vows #5 22

Basic Vows #6 23

Ceremonies without Clergy or
Officiant 16

Childhood Sweethearts 52

Civil Ceremonies 15

Closing Words 13

Conventional Vows 24–29

Conventional Vows #1 24

Conventional Vows #2 25

Conventional Vows #3 26

Conventional Vows #4 27

Conventional Vows #5 27

Conventional Vows #6 28

Conventional Vows #7 29

Episcopal Church, Exchange
of Vows 36

From Friends to Lovers 50

High School Sweethearts 57

I Do, I Do, I Do 84

I Would Do It Over Again . . .83

Introduction 6–7

Lutheran Vows 36

Nondenominational Christian
Vows 35

Nondenominational
Vows #1 30

Nondenominational
Vows #2 31

Nondenominational
Vows #3 32–33

Nondenominational
Vows #4 34

Nontraditional Vows 44–48

Nontraditional Vows #1 44

Nontraditional Vows #2 45

Nontraditional Vows #3 46

Nontraditional Vows #4 47

Nontraditional Vows #5 48

Not Looking for Love 55

Opening Words 10

Personal Vows 49–57

Question of Intent 11

Readings 85–92

Reading for a Church
Setting 60

Religious Ceremonies 14

Renewing Your Vows 82–84

Silver Threads Among
the Gold 56

Spring Reading 67

Spring Vows 66

Summary 93

Summer Reading 69
Summer Vows 68
Surprised by Love 54

The Announcement or
    Declaration 13
The Blessing 12–13
The Dance of Life 51
The Exchange of Rings 12
The Readings 10–11
The Vows 11–12
The Wedding
    Ceremony 8–13
To the Seasons 65
Traditional Religious
    Vows 36–37
Traditional Religious
    Vows #1 37

Vows 17–84
Vows for a Church
    Setting 58–60
Vows for a Church
    Setting #1 58
Vows for a Church
    Setting #2 59
Vows for a Home Setting 61
Vows for a Home Setting #1 ..61
Vows for a Mountain
    Wedding 64
Vows for Outdoor
    Ceremonies 62–64
Vows for Outdoor
    Ceremonies #1 62
Vows for Outdoor
    Ceremonies #2 63
Vows for Second
    Marriages 75–77
Vows for Second
    Marriages #1 75

Vows for Second
    Marriages #2 76
Vows for Second
    Marriages #3 77
Vows for the Season 65–73
Vows Including Family
    Members 78–81
Vows Inspired from Literature
    and the Bible 38–43
Vows Inspired #1 38
Vows Inspired #2 39
Vows Inspired #3 39
Vows Inspired #4 40
Vows Inspired #5 40
Vows Inspired #6 40
Vows Inspired #7 41
Vows Inspired #8 41
Vows Inspired #9 42
Vows Inspired #10 42
Vows Inspired #11 43
Vows Inspired #12 43
Vows to Fit Wedding
    Venues 19
Vows to Include
    Children 71–73
Vows to Include
    Children #1 78
Vows to Include
    Children #2 79
Vows to Include Children
    Reading #1 80
Vows to Include Children
    Reading #2 80
Vows to Include Parents 81
Vows, Words, and
    Meanings 18

Wedding Feast Vows 74
Winter Reading 73
Winter Vows 72